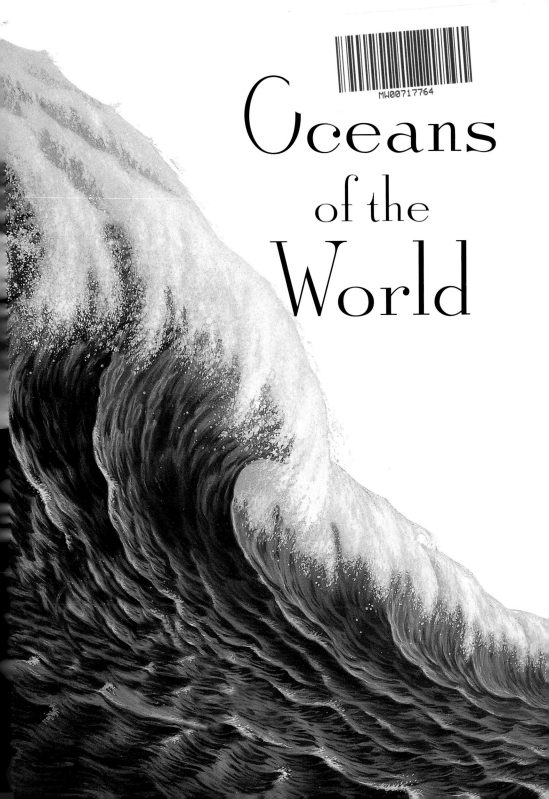

Oceans
of the
World

Contents

Features

How might oceans carry an object from one country to another? See for yourself on page 6.

Do you know that the *Titanic* sank in 1912 and the wreckage wasn't found until 1985? Turn to page 13 to discover who finally found the sunken ship.

What do the words *salary*, meaning a worker's pay, and *salt* have in common? Turn to page 21 to find out.

One of the world's most valuable gems is grown in the ocean. Find out which one in **Planting a Seed** on page 24.

Who was Jacques Cousteau?

Visit www.rigbyinfoquest.com
for more about OCEANS.

A World of Water

The name of our planet and a word for soil may be the same, but more than two-thirds of Earth is covered in saltwater. There are four large areas of saltwater called oceans—the Pacific, the Atlantic, the Indian, and the Arctic—and many smaller areas called seas. The Pacific Ocean is the largest and deepest. It covers 32 percent of Earth's surface.

Oceans affect air temperature and supply moisture for rain. They provide us with food, **resources**, and a vast watery world to explore and study.

Oceans of the World

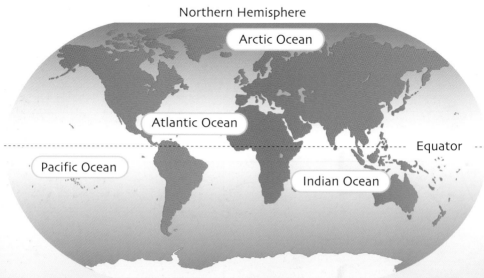

Northern Hemisphere

Arctic Ocean

Atlantic Ocean

Equator

Pacific Ocean

Indian Ocean

Southern Hemisphere

Almost all the water on Earth is saltwater. Less than 3 percent is freshwater, and most of this is frozen in ice caps and glaciers. Only about 1 percent is in rivers, lakes, and underground channels.

Currents and Tides

Ocean movement is caused by currents and tides. Currents are large, moving streams of water caused by winds blowing on the surfaces of the oceans. Warm water is sometimes moved to colder parts of the world by large, circular currents, and cold water is sometimes moved to warmer parts of the world.

FAST FACTS

Currents of the World

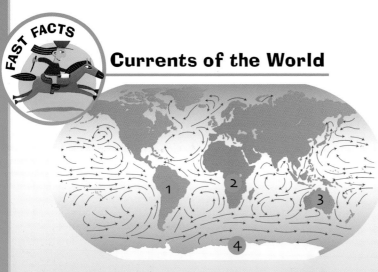

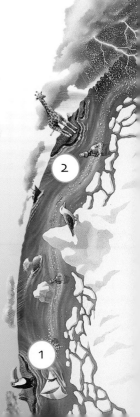

In an experiment, twenty bottles were thrown from a ship that was traveling between South America and Antarctica. It took over two years for ocean currents to carry the bottles to Australia and New Zealand. Can you find the currents between South America and Australia on the map above?

6

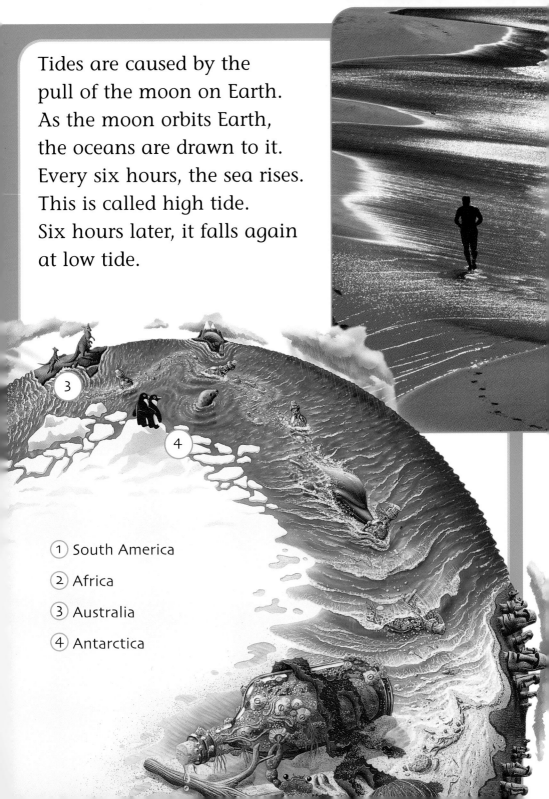

Tides are caused by the pull of the moon on Earth. As the moon orbits Earth, the oceans are drawn to it. Every six hours, the sea rises. This is called high tide. Six hours later, it falls again at low tide.

1. South America
2. Africa
3. Australia
4. Antarctica

The Coasts

Settlements

For thousands of years, people have settled along the coasts of oceans and seas. Shipping was the main way of getting goods to other countries. Traders often made long and dangerous journeys. They traveled to many parts of the world to trade goods.

Today, more than half the world's population lives on or near coasts. Many people live in large cities with ports. Some ports are in natural harbors formed by bays or the mouths of large rivers. Others are in harbors that have been specially made.

The U.S. city of San Francisco, California is built on land by a natural harbor.

Over 2,000 years ago, the port of Piraeus in Greece was a leading trade center. One large **import** was grain. Honey and silver were among the **exports.**

9

Protecting the Coasts

Many countries make laws to protect their coastal resources, especially fish. Most countries control an area of ocean from their coasts and out to sea for 200 miles. Agreements are made and **treaties** are signed to protect coastal waters around the world.

The Changing Coasts

Coasts are always changing shape. Powerful waves break down rock, and strong winds and sea currents carry rock and sand out to sea or to other parts of the coast. Some coasts are worn away while others are built up.

Eroded coast

Lighthouses are found on coasts around the world. They are used to guide ships, warning of land, rocks, or reefs near the coast. Lighthouses look different and have different signals. This is so sailors can use the location of a lighthouse to help figure out their ship's position in an ocean.

Exploring the Unknown

Today's high-tech research ships and **submersibles** make it possible for scientists to go deeper and learn more about oceans than ever before. The scientists study sea animals, currents, and the land that makes up the ocean floors. They study how oceans affect climate and weather around the world.

Most submersibles carry one or two people and are attached to a research ship. Robot submersibles explore very deep waters and narrow places where people cannot go.

Research ship

PROFILE

DR. ROBERT BALLARD

Dr. Robert Ballard is a U.S. scientist and ocean explorer at Woods Hole in Massachusetts. Many of his expeditions have led to great discoveries. Some of these are:

- (1973–74) a huge underwater mountain range in the Atlantic Ocean, larger than any mountain range on land

- (1977) underwater hot springs and strange animal life never seen before off the coast of Ecuador in South America

- (1979) black smokers, or underwater volcanoes, off the coast of California in the United States

- (1985) the wreckage of the ship *Titanic*, which sank in 1912 after hitting an iceberg in the Atlantic Ocean

A submersible was sent inside the wreckage of the *Titanic* to take photos.

13

Beneath the Surface

Beneath the surface of each ocean lies land that is similar to land above sea level. It has volcanoes, valleys, slopes, plains, trenches, and ridges. The largest ocean trench is nearly 36,000 feet below sea level. It's deeper than the height of Mount Everest, the highest mountain on land.

Scientists use sound waves to measure underwater land formations. By measuring how long it takes sound waves to bounce back to their instruments, scientists can make maps of ocean floors.

Using submersibles, scientists can find black smokers on ocean floors. The smokers spurt hot water and black smoke.

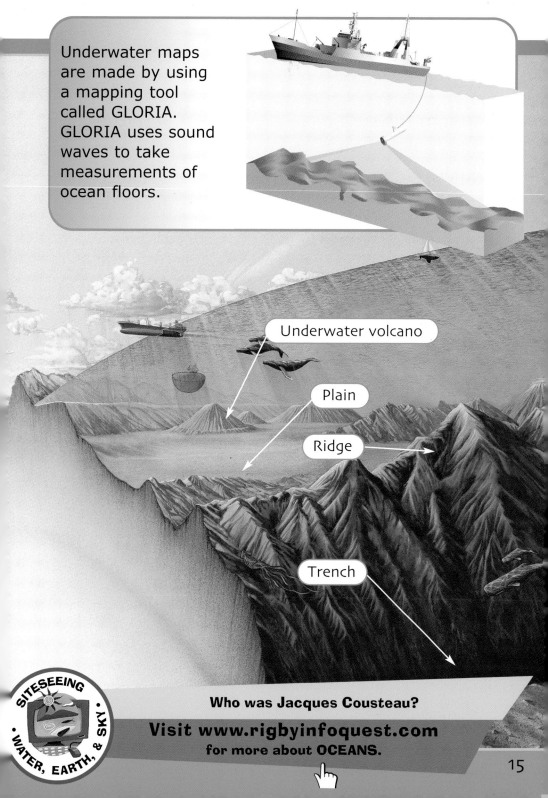

Underwater maps are made by using a mapping tool called GLORIA. GLORIA uses sound waves to take measurements of ocean floors.

Underwater volcano

Plain

Ridge

Trench

Who was Jacques Cousteau?

Visit www.rigbyinfoquest.com
for more about **OCEANS.**

SITESEEING · WATER, EARTH, & SKY ·

There are three main kinds of life found
in the oceans. Tiny plants and animals
that drift in the currents are called plankton.
There are animals that swim, such as fish and
whales. Finally, there are creatures that live
on or near ocean floors, such as worms
and sponges.

The oceans provide food for all the creatures living
in them. Each creature feeds on plants or other
animals, so it is like a link in a chain. This is
called a **food chain.** A change in just one link
affects all the other creatures in the chain.

Large ocean creatures such as some whales and sharks eat fish and seals. Fish and seals eat small fish, and small fish eat plankton. Each creature is a link in the food chain.

Harvesting the Oceans

Fishy Food

Fish are an important source of food for many people. As the world's population increases, fishing businesses grow and provide food and jobs for millions of people.

Most saltwater fish are caught in waters near coasts. These areas are known as **commercial fishing zones.** Large fishing boats use different kinds of nets to catch fish. Many fishing boats have gear on board to prepare their catches for sale.

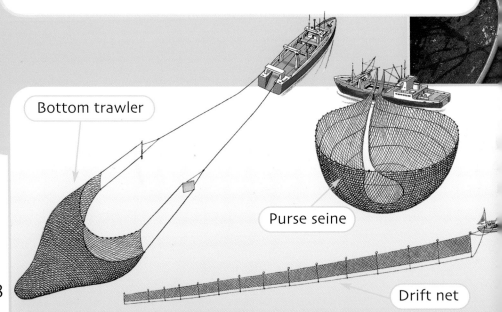

Bottom trawler

Purse seine

Drift net

Where Are the World's Fish Caught?

- Pacific Ocean
- Atlantic Ocean
- Indian Ocean
- Inland freshwater

Drift-Net Fishing

A drift net is a rectangular net measuring up to 3 miles long. Drift nets have been banned in oceans since 1993. Drift nets catch many fish, but they also trap and kill creatures such as dolphins, seals, turtles, and whales. Other nets, such as bottom trawlers and purse seines, are still used.

A Salty Harvest

Around the world, over 230 million tons of salt are harvested every year. The source of all salt is brine, or salty water, from oceans and seas. Even salt found underground was formed by the **evaporation** of oceans millions of years ago.

Chemical businesses use most of the world's salt harvest to produce chemicals. Only 4 percent of the total salt harvest is eaten in food!

Salt is harvested by evaporating saltwater in places where there is plenty of sunshine.

WORD BUILDER

The word *salary* (a worker's pay) comes from the Latin word for salt—*salarium*. This is because soldiers in Ancient Rome were often paid salt, not money.

Farming the Oceans

Some coastal areas are set up as "sea farms." The Chinese have been fish farming for thousands of years. Seaweed and shellfish such as oysters, shrimps, and mussels are also often grown and harvested on "farms."

Oyster farm

Oyster farms are usually found in waters that are rich in algae—an oyster's natural food. Oysters are grown in trays or on sticks. They are usually harvested after they have been growing for 18 months to 3 years. Almost all oysters that are sold as food come from oyster farms.

There are about 7,000 kinds of seaweed! Seaweed has many uses, and is rich in vitamins and minerals. Seaweed is an important ingredient in Japanese food called sushi.

Planting a Seed

A pearl is a valuable gem that grows inside the shell of an oyster. Today, most pearls are grown in ocean farms along warm coastal waters. To grow a pearl, a tiny piece of another kind of shell is placed inside a three-year-old oyster. The oyster is then returned to the sea. The pearl grows as layers of a substance called nacre build up around the seed shell.

1 A tiny piece of shell is placed inside each oyster.

2 The oysters are returned to the sea.

3 The oysters are cleaned regularly.

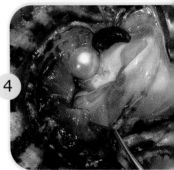

4 A valuable pearl is harvested.

The oysters are moved and cleaned twice a year to make sure they have the best growing conditions. When the shells are opened between one and three years later, only about one in every twenty oysters contains a pearl.

Diving for Pearls

Long ago, pearls were gathered by divers who were tied by ropes to a boat. The divers had to hold their breath because there was no breathing equipment then.

Mining for Oil

One of the most valuable resources from the ocean is oil. Oil is used to generate nearly half the energy used in the world. Oil is found deep underground—on land and at sea. Huge offshore oil platforms, or rigs, are used to explore beneath the ocean floors for oil.

Up to fifty different wells can be drilled from a single platform to collect millions of barrels of oil each day. Most offshore oil rigs are used for about twenty-five years.

What Is Oil?

Oil is made when dead plants and animals sink to the bottom of the ocean. Over thousands of years, the dead matter is buried and squashed between layers of rock. The pressure from the rock slowly turns the dead matter into oil.

Hundreds of workers live on an oil rig for weeks at a time. A helicopter is often used to take workers to and from an oil rig.

Oceans of Fun

Oceans can be fun for people of all ages. There are many ocean sports to take part in. Near coasts, people can swim, surf, windsurf, and water-ski. Further out in the ocean, people can go deep-sea fishing and diving.

Exploring different parts of the ocean is also fun. A coastline can be packed with shells, rocks, and small creatures such as crabs. A shallow reef can have beautiful **coral** and fish of many colors.

Fun on the Water

Waterskiing is a fast, exciting sport. Water-skiers race across an ocean's surface behind a speedboat, twisting and turning. In a strong wind, a windsurfer can also be quite speedy. Sailing can be a much slower, relaxing activity or a serious sporting race.

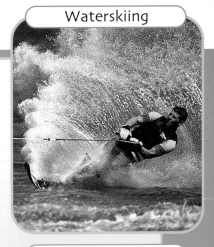
Waterskiing

Windsurfing

Sailing

Glossary

commercial fishing zone – an area of ocean where fish are caught for the purpose of selling

coral – a hard, stony substance that is found in shallow parts of warm oceans. Coral is the combined skeletons of tiny sea creatures.

evaporation – the process in which a liquid changes into a vapor or a gas. Water evaporates when it is boiled.

export – a product that is sold and sent to another country

food chain – a pathway of food supply. In the ocean, a food chain starts with plankton that is eaten by some kinds of fish. These fish then become food for other kinds of fish.

import – a product that is bought and brought in from another country

resource – something from nature that is available for people to use. Ocean resources include fish, salt, shellfish, seaweed, and oil.

submersible – a small submarine that can go as deep as seven miles beneath an ocean's surface

treaty – a written agreement between two or more countries, often about trading and cooperation

Index

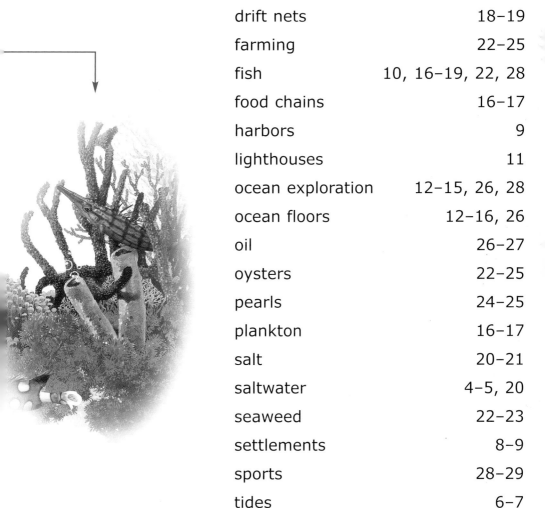

Discussion Starters

1 Oceans can be great fun when you're swimming, fishing, boating, or surfing. However, there are also dangers. What dangers should you be aware of when you're swimming or when you're boating? What kind of safety equipment would you need on a boat?

2 Drift-net fishing has been banned around the world because large drift nets trap and kill many sea creatures needlessly. Do you agree or disagree with this ban? Why do you think other nets can still be used?

3 There are many different ways to study an ocean. Some scientists study what happens on the surface of an ocean, some study life in an ocean, and others study the floor of an ocean. Which part of an ocean would you most like to study? Why?